FACT CAT

MAMMALS

Izzi Howell

D1420757

WAYLAND
www.waylandbooks.co.uk

FACT CAT

Get your paws on this fantastic new mega-series from Wayland!

Join our Fact Cat on a journey of fun learning about every subject under the sun!

First published in Great Britain in 2015 by Wayland
Copyright © Wayland 2015

ISBN: 978 0 7502 9598 7
Dewey Number: 599-dc23

10 9 8 7 6 5 4 3 2 1

MIX
Paper from responsible sources
FSC® C104740

Wayland
An imprint of Hachette Children's Group
Part of Hodder & Stoughton
Carmelite House
50 Victoria Embankment
London EC4Y 0DZ

An Hachette UK Company
www.hachette.co.uk
www.hachettechildrens.co.uk

A catalogue for this title is available from the British Library
Printed and bound in China

Produced for Wayland by
White-Thomson Publishing Ltd
www.wtpub.co.uk

Editor: Izzi Howell
Design: Clare Nicholas
Fact Cat illustrations: Shutterstock/Julien Troneur
Other illustrations: Stefan Chabluk
Consultant: Kate Ruttle

Picture and illustration credits:
Corbis: DLILLC 5; iStock: falun 8, triggerfishsaul 9, DmitryND 10t, brianhumek 12, guioo878 15, Wildroze 18, JohnCarnemolla 21; Shutterstock: Cynthia Kidwell (cover), john michael evan potter (title page), Karen H. Ilagan 4, c.byatt-norman 6, Nicram Sabod 7, Mogens Trolle 10b, Tania Thomson 11, Kjuuurs 13, Volodymyr Burdiak 14t, hammett79 14b, john michael evan potter 16, Elena Blokhina 17, enciktat 19, Ivan Kuzmin 20.

Every effort has been made to clear copyright. Should there be any inadvertent omission, please apply to the publisher for rectification.

The author, Izzi Howell, is a writer and editor specialising in children's educational publishing.

The consultant, Kate Ruttle, is a literacy expert and SENCO, and teaches in Suffolk.

FACT CAT FACT

There is a question for you to answer on each spread in this book. You can check your answers on page 24.

CONTENTS

WHAT IS A MAMMAL?

Mammals are a group of animals that are similar to each other in certain ways. Most mammals have four legs and are covered in hair or **fur**. Nearly all mammals give birth to **live young**, rather than laying eggs.

Humans and hamsters are both examples of mammals.

Mammals are the cleverest animals on Earth. They have large brains and they can learn new things. Some mammals even use tools to make everyday tasks easier.

Chimpanzees use sticks to pick insects out of nests and tree trunks. Can you find out which other mammals use tools?

FACT CAT FACT

There are more than 5,000 types of mammal in the world. They are found on every **continent**.

HABITATS

Most mammals live on land. Mammals can live in cold and hot **habitats** because they are **warm-blooded**. Warm-blooded animals can warm themselves up by **shivering** or cool themselves down by **sweating**.

In hot weather, dogs cool down by **panting** to lose heat from their bodies.

FACT CAT FACT

It's difficult for cats to sweat through their thick fur, so they sweat the most on the soles of their feet! This area isn't covered in fur, so it's easier to lose heat from there.

A few types of mammal live in oceans and rivers. Some **aquatic** mammals, such as whales and dolphins, spend all their time in the water. **Semi-aquatic** mammals, such as seals, live on land and in the water.

Grey seals spend most of their time hunting for fish in the sea but they come on to land to give birth. What is the young of a seal called?

BREATHING

All mammals need to breathe air, whether they live on land or in the water. When mammals breathe in, their **lungs** take **oxygen** from the air and help to send it around their bodies.

The moose, like most mammals, can breathe through its nose or its mouth.

Aquatic mammals swim to the **surface** of the water to breathe air. They have large lungs that can store a lot of air, which means they can hold their breath for a long time underwater.

blowhole

Dolphins and whales breathe through a hole on top of their head called a blowhole.

FUR

Fur keeps mammals warm in cold habitats. It can also act as **camouflage**. When animals are the same colour as their habitat, it is harder for **predators** to see them.

This Arctic fox has white fur, which is the same colour as its snowy habitat. Which other mammals have white fur?

The light brown colour of a meerkat's fur helps it to hide in its sandy African habitat.

Aquatic mammals, such as whales and dolphins, have no fur. These animals have smooth skin that allows them to move easily through water. Semi-aquatic mammals, such as otters and beavers, have **waterproof** fur.

Beavers have oily fur that doesn't **absorb** water. If their fur absorbed water, they would be too heavy to swim.

FACT CAT FACT

An adult sea otter has up to 800 million hairs on its body! Sea otters need thick fur to keep warm in the water.

YOUNG

Young mammals grow inside their mother's **womb**. Small mammals, such as rats, have a shorter **pregnancy** than large mammals, such as elephants.

Horses are usually pregnant with only one **foal** at a time.

FACT CAT FACT

Rats are only pregnant for around 21 days before their babies are born, whereas elephants are pregnant for around two years! How much does a baby elephant weigh when it is born?

Kangaroos keep their **joeys** in a pouch on their front until the joeys are big enough to move by themselves.

joey

Female mammals give birth to live young. Young mammals drink milk from their mother until they are ready to eat **solid** food. Mothers teach their young how to find food and keep safe.

FOOD

Carnivores eat animals that they have hunted and killed, so they have sharp front teeth for tearing meat. **Herbivores** only eat plants, so they have wide flat teeth to cut leaves into smaller pieces.

Leopards use their sharp front teeth to kill and eat monkeys and other large mammals.

Zebras chew grass with their wide flat teeth.

Omnivores eat both animals and plants. The diet of an omnivore changes throughout the year, depending on what kind of food they can find. For example, raccoons eat insects in spring, but in autumn, they eat berries.

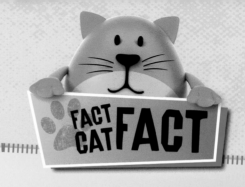

Red pandas are omnivores. They mainly feed on bamboo, but they also eat small mammals. Which continent do red pandas live on?

SENSES

Mammals have five senses - sight, sound, smell, taste and touch. These senses give mammals information about the world around them.

Bats use sound to find out what is around them. They make clicking noises that **echo** off nearby objects. This type of echo tells the bat how close the object is. Which other mammal uses sound in the same way?

The African elephant has the best sense of smell of any animal. They can smell water from nearly 20 kilometres away.

Herbivores, such as horses, often have eyes on the sides of their heads, which gives them a better view of what is around them. This means that they will quickly see if a predator is approaching.

These two pictures show how a herbivore and a carnivore would see the same area of land. The herbivore can see a much wider area than the carnivore.

how a herbivore sees

how a carnivore sees

MOVEMENT

Mammals can move on land, in trees, in water and under the ground. On land, most mammals walk and run on four legs. Some mammals can climb high into trees, using their strong back legs to move up the tree trunk.

This howler monkey is using its tail to hang from a branch. Some monkeys can use their hands to hold things, just like humans can.

FACT CAT FACT

The cheetah is the world's fastest land mammal. It can go from standing still to moving at 96km an hour in only three seconds. What is the slowest land mammal?

In the water, aquatic mammals use their **flippers** to push themselves forwards. Most land mammals can also swim for a short amount of time.

Big cats, such as tigers, are excellent swimmers. They catch animals such as fish in rivers, and carry them through the water to eat on land.

STRANGE MAMMALS

Bats are strange mammals. They have wings and they can fly like birds. But unlike birds, bats have fur and give birth to live young.

Bat wings are thin and **delicate**. If bats had thick wings, they would be too heavy to fly.

Australian platypuses are one of very few mammals that don't give birth to live young. Female platypuses lay eggs in an underground nest, and cover them to keep them warm. After 10 days, young platypuses hatch from the eggs.

Platypuses have **webbed** feet and beaks like ducks, so they are sometimes called 'duck-billed' platypuses.

FACT CAT FACT

Male platypuses have **venomous** spikes on their ankles! The venom isn't strong enough to kill a human, but it could kill a dog. Can you find out the name of another venomous mammal?

QUIZ

Try to answer the questions below. Look back through the book to help you. Check your answers on page 24.

1 Aquatic mammals live on land. True or not true?

a) true

b) not true

2 Which mammal breathes through a blowhole?

a) sheep

b) tiger

c) dolphin

3 Young mammals grow inside their mother's womb. True or not true?

a) true

b) not true

4 Which type of animal only eats meat?

a) carnivore

b) herbivore

c) omnivore

5 What is the fastest land mammal?

a) elephant

b) cheetah

c) horse

6 Bats can fly. True or not true?

a) true

b) not true

GLOSSARY

absorb to take in liquid and keep it in

aquatic describes something that lives in water

camouflage a way of hiding by being the same colour as the area you are in

carnivore an animal that only eats meat

continent one of the seven main areas of land on Earth, such as Africa

delicate easily broken

echo if a sound echoes, you hear it again

female an animal that can get pregnant and give birth to young

flipper a paddle-shaped body part that aquatic animals use for swimming

foal a horse's young

fur hair that covers some mammals

habitat the area where a plant or an animal lives

herbivore an animal that only eats plants

joey a kangaroo's young

live describes something that is alive

lung a body part that is used for breathing

omnivore an animal that eats meat and plants

oxygen a gas in the air that animals need to breathe to live

pant to breathe with your mouth open and your tongue out

predator an animal that kills and eats animals

pregnancy the period of time when a female mammal has her young growing in her womb

semi-aquatic something that lives on land and in water

shiver to shake because you are cold

solid something that isn't a liquid or a gas

surface the top part of something

sweat to produce liquid from your skin

venomous describes an animal whose body produces poison

warm-blooded describes an animal that can keep its body temperature the same regardless of its surroundings

waterproof something that does not let water through

webbed when toes or fingers are joined together by skin

womb a part of the female body where young grows until it is ready to be born

young an animal's babies

23

INDEX

ANSWERS

Pages 4–21

Page 5: Some examples include sea otters and orangutans.

Page 7: A seal pup

Page 9: They have a long nose that looks like an elephant's trunk.

Page 10: Some examples include polar bears and Arctic hares.

Page 12: Around 90 kilograms

Page 15: Asia

Page 16: Dolphins

Page 18: Sloths

Page 21: Some examples include vampire bats and shrews.

Quiz answers

1   not true – they live in the water.
2   c - dolphin
3   true
4   a – carnivore
5   b – cheetah
6   true

OTHER TITLES IN THE FACT CAT SERIES...

WAYLAND
www.waylandbooks.co.uk